Sound, Heat & Light: Energy At Work

by Melvin Berger

illustrated by Anna DiVito

SCHOLASTIC INC.
New York Toronto London Auckland Sydney

Prrr....
Prr rr......
Prrrr

Text copyright © 1992 by Melvin Berger.
Illustrations copyright © 1992 by Scholastic Inc.
All rights reserved. Published by Scholastic Inc.
Printed in the U.S.A.
ISBN 0-590-46103-6

Clap your hands. Hear the sound.
Stand near a stove. Feel the heat.
Turn on a lamp. See the light.

Sound, heat, and light.
How different they are.
Yet how alike.
They are all forms of energy.

Play your radio very loudly.
The sound energy hurts your ears.
Talk into a telephone.
The sound energy sends your
voice many miles.

Heat energy from the sun melts snow and ice.
Heat energy from a stove changes raw meat into
a tasty hamburger.

Light energy helps plants grow.
Light energy darkens the film inside a camera.

Sound, heat, and light are all forms of energy.
But they are alike in another important way.

They are three great topics of science!

Sound

Listen! What sounds do you hear?
    People talking?
    Someone playing the guitar?
    A buzzing fly?
    A ringing telephone?

All these sounds are made the same way.
Something is shaking back and forth very fast.
When something is shaking very fast we say
it is vibrating.

People talking?
Their vocal cords are vibrating.

Someone playing the guitar?
The guitar strings are vibrating.

A fly buzzing?
The insect's wings are beating very fast.

A ringing telephone?
The bell inside is vibrating.

Vibrations produce sound.
You can see it happen.

Get a rubber band.
Stretch it between your hands.

Now pluck the rubber band.
Do you hear the sound?
Do you see it shaking back and forth?

The rubber band is vibrating.
The vibrations make the sound.

You can also feel vibrations.
Lightly touch the front of your throat.
Say your name or count to ten.
Do you feel the vibrations?
They come from your vibrating vocal cords.

Some sounds are very loud.
The loudest sound of all was made by the
volcano Krakatoa.
Krakatoa erupted in 1883.
The noise could be heard 3,000 miles away!

What is the loudest sound you have ever heard?
>A jet plane flying low?
>A rock music concert?
>A big truck roaring by?

You can't make as much noise as an exploding volcano.
Nor can you roar like a jet plane.
But you can make some very loud noises.

Hit a metal can with a stick.
Drop an old pot on a hard floor.
Shout at the top of your lungs.
These are very loud sounds.

You can also make soft sounds.
Tap gently on a table.
Whisper your name.
Rub your face.
These sounds are very soft.
Some may be even too soft to hear.

Can you think of other soft sounds?
   A cat's meow?
   Raindrops falling on a roof or window?
   Someone humming?

Sounds are either loud or soft.
They can also be either low or high.

You can make low sounds.
Growl like a lion.
Make the sound deep and rumbling.
Thunder and tubas also make very low sounds.

What other low sounds can you think of?

Now make a very high sound.
It may even sound squeaky.
A crying baby and a flute also make high sounds.
Can you think of other high sounds?

You can make low and high sounds with your voice.
The sounds come from two vocal cords in your throat.
They are inside a voice box made of cartilage.
Sometimes we call it an Adam's apple.
It feels like a bump on your throat.

Each vocal cord is a tiny layer of flesh.
To talk or sing you blow air through the cords.
They vibrate.
The vibrating vocal cords make the sound of your voice.

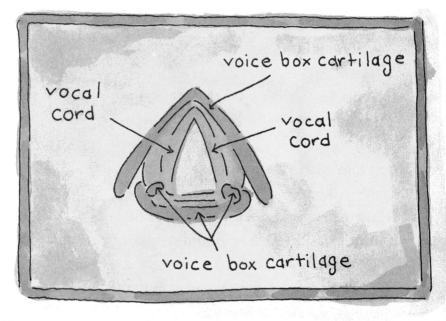

Suppose you sing a low note.
Your Adam's apple moves down.
The vocal cords become loose and flabby.
You blow air through them.
They vibrate slowly.
Out comes a low note.

Try it.
Lightly touch your Adam's apple.
Now sing a low note.
Do you feel your voice box move down?

Suppose now you sing a high note.
Your Adam's apple moves up.
The vocal cords become tight and stiff.
The moving air makes them vibrate very fast.
The sound is high and screechy.

Try it.
Keep your hand on your Adam's apple.
Sing a high note.
Do you feel your Adam's apple jump up?

When you talk or sing your vocal cords vibrate.
The vibrations make the air vibrate.
The vibrating air forms a sound wave.

The sound wave spreads out to all sides.
Forward and back.
Right and left.
Up and down, too.

A sound wave is much like a water wave.
Drop a stone into a pond or a bathtub.
It makes a wave.
The wave spreads out.
It forms bigger and bigger circles.

Sound waves are a little different.
You can't see them.
You can only hear them.

Also, sound waves go off in all directions.
Water waves stay mostly on top of the water.

As sound waves spread out they sometimes
bump into a wall.
The sound wave bounces back.
You hear the sound again.
It is called an echo.

Shout your name in an empty gym.
Or try it in a tile bathroom.
Listen for the echo.

You hear the echo for a good reason.
It takes time for sound to get from one
place to another.
But sound moves through the air very fast.
It zips along at about 740 miles an hour!

Some airplanes fly faster than sound.
Their speed is over 740 miles an hour.
These airplanes are called supersonic.

The *Concorde* is the most famous
supersonic airplane.
It can reach speeds up to 1,450 miles an hour!
That is nearly twice as fast as sound.

Now you know a lot about sound.
Sound is a form of energy.
Sound is made by vibrations.
Sound can be loud or soft, low or high.

But what happens to sounds once they are made?

Suppose you shout "Hello" to a friend.
Your voice is high and loud.

The vibrations reach your friend's ears.
They pass to the eardrum inside the ear.
They make the eardrum start to vibrate.

The vibrating eardrum sends a signal to
your friend's brain.
The brain decides what the sound means.
Your friend answers, "Hello."
And the sound's journey is over!

Heat

You and I need heat energy
- from heaters to keep us cozy.
- from stoves to cook our food.
- from burning fuel to run our cars.

Adding heat energy makes things warmer.
You buy a can of beans in the store.
Then you put the beans on the stove.
Heat energy from the stove warms the beans.
Now they are ready to eat.

Taking heat energy away makes things cooler.
You buy some apples.
Then you put them in the refrigerator.
The cold refrigerator takes heat energy out
of the fruit.
The apples taste cold and delicious.

One way to add heat energy is with a fire.
A fire in the oil or gas burner warms most homes.
A fire in a gas oven or grill cooks your dinner.
Tiny fires in car and plane engines make them run.

Rubbing also produces heat energy.
Adults rub a match on something rough.
Rubbing heats the match.
The heat makes the match burst into flame.

Native Americans long ago didn't have matches.
Instead they rubbed two sticks together.
Rubbing made the sticks very hot.
The heat set the sticks on fire.

Imagine it is a cold, frosty day.
Your hands are icy.
You rub them together very hard and fast.
The heat energy makes them feel warmer.

Pressing down also produces heat energy.
You can see how this works.

Get a fork and an ice cube.
Press the fork on the ice cube.
Hold it there for a few minutes.

Take the fork away.
Do you see where it melted the ice cube?

The heat from pressing can be useful.
It makes ice skating possible.
Your weight presses on the blade.
The blade presses on the ice.
A thin layer of water forms on top of the ice.
It lets you skate—or slide—through the water.

But the heat from pressing may cause an accident.
Suppose a car drives over a patch of ice.
The weight of the car forms a layer of water
on the ice.
The car skids out of control.

Most objects grow bigger when they are heated.
Rocket engines burn fuel.
The burning fuel produces hot gases.

The hot gases grow bigger.
They need more space.
The gases push against the front of the engine.
They send the rocket flying forward at high speed.

Automobiles burn gasoline in their engines.
The burning gasoline forms hot gases.
The hot gases push against parts of the engine.
These parts go up and down.
They turn the wheels to make the car go.

a view
of an
automobile
engine

Adding heat may change objects altogether.
Put an ice cream cone in the heat of the sun.
What happens?

The sun adds heat energy to the ice cream.
It gets softer and softer.
The solid ice cream becomes a soupy liquid.

The opposite is also true.
Taking heat away from an object may
also change it.
Put an ice cube tray in a freezer.
What happens?

The freezer takes heat away from the water.
The water turns to ice.
The liquid water becomes solid ice.

We measure the heat in an object with a thermometer.
The thermometer is a thin glass tube.
Marks on the tube show the degrees of temperature.

At the bottom of the glass tube is a round bulb.
The bulb is filled with a liquid.

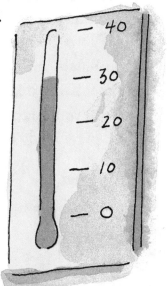

Suppose you heat the liquid.
It grows bigger.
Where can it go?
Up the thin glass tube.
The hotter the liquid,
the higher it goes.
The mark it reaches is the
temperature in degrees.

Say you feel sick.
Your mother or father wants to take your temperature.
First, your parent shakes the thermometer.
This knocks all the liquid down into the bulb.

Then he or she places the bulb end under your tongue.
The heat of your body warms the liquid.
It grows too big for the glass bulb.
The liquid rises in the tube.

After a few minutes you take out the thermometer.
Your mom or dad looks closely at the numbers.
How high did the liquid go?

Did it reach 98.6 degrees?
    Your body temperature is normal.
Did it reach 100 degrees?
    You have a mild fever.
Did it reach 101 degrees or more?
    You have a high fever.
    You may need to see a doctor.

Feet may get bigger with heat.
Did you know that?

You wake up in the morning.
Your feet are cool.
All day you walk around in sneakers or shoes.
Your feet get hotter and hotter.
They also get bigger and bigger.

The heat makes your feet bigger.
But the sneakers stay about the same size.
That's when your feet start to hurt.

Some people say you should only buy
shoes in the afternoon.
Can you guess why?

Heat also travels through solid objects.
Think of someone cooking soup.
The pot is on the stove.
It gets very hot.

The pot handle sticks out to the side.
It is not near the heat.
Yet the heat travels from the pot to the handle.
Touch the handle and you may burn your hand.

Heat does not travel easily through wood.
One end of a wooden match may be burning.
The other end is not even warm.

Heat also travels through liquids.
Let's say you put a pot of cold water on a hot stove.
The stove heats the bottom of the pot.
The hot pot warms the lowest layer of water.

The warm water moves up.
It makes the rest of the water hotter and hotter.
In a few minutes all the water is boiling.

Heat can be dangerous.
    It can start fires.
    It can cause blisters.
    It can make cars skid.

But heat can also be very helpful.
    It keeps us warm.
    It cooks our food.
    It runs our cars and planes.

If we are careful, heat can be a wonderful helper!

Light

Most of our light comes from the sun.
Sunlight is very, very bright.
It gives as much light as two billion,
billion, BILLION candles!

By day we play and work in
the bright sunlight.
At night it is dark.
We can't see the sun.

On some nights we can see the light of the moon.
Do you know what makes moonlight?

The moon itself has no light.
Moonlight is the sun's light bouncing off the moon.

Moonlight is not nearly as bright as sunlight.
So people have always tried to get more light at night.

At first fires helped them to see in the dark.
Outdoors they built big campfires.
Indoors they made fires in stone fireplaces.
Flaming wood torches helped them get from
place to place.

Candles came a little later.
They are made of thick cords called wicks.

Candle makers set the wick into wax.
You light the top of the wick.
The flame gives off a clear, bright light.

Oil lamps were another way to get light.
An oil lamp has a wick, too.
The bottom of the wick rests in a bowl of oil.

You light the top end of the wick.
It burns with a good, steady light.
The lamp gives light as long as there is oil.

Today electric lamps give us light.
Some light comes from bulbs.
The bulbs may be on the ceiling or a wall.
Or they may be in a lamp.

It's easy to turn on these bulbs.
You flip a switch.
The bulb lights.

Flipping the switch lets electricity flow.
It flows to the bulb.
Inside the bulb is a very thin length of wire.
The electricity passes through the wire.
The wire grows very hot.

The very hot wire glows a bright white.
Now you have light.

Not all electric lights use bulbs.
Some use long, skinny tubes.
These lights are called fluorescent.

Flip the switch.
The electricity flows.
It flows through the fluorescent tube.
The inside of the fluorescent tube is lined
with a chemical.

Electricity makes this chemical glow.
You have light.

Fluorescent lights are better than bulbs.
They use less electricity.
They give off more light.
And they don't get as hot.

Right now you're reading this book.
Where does the light come from?
    The sun?
    An electric light?

Either way, the light strikes the book.
It bounces off the book.
And you see that light.

In some ways, light is like a ball.
Throw it against a wall.
The ball bounces back.

Shine light on a book—or wall—and it bounces back.
Such light is called reflected light.

Reflected light from a book lets you read the book.
Reflected light from a tree lets you see the tree.
Reflected light from a face lets you look at the face.

What happens to the reflected light from the book?
Some goes into your eyes.
Your eyes send signals to your brain.
Your brain lets you read and understand the words.

Mirrors reflect light very well.
Most mirrors are flat pieces of glass.
Behind the glass is a thin layer
of shiny metal.

Light passes through the glass.
It strikes the metal.
The metal reflects back the light.
It lets you see your face in the mirror.

Have you ever seen a rainbow in the sky?
What about rainbow colors
- in a piece of glass?
- in soap bubbles?
- in a water spray?

Most light is white light.
But white light is made up of many colors.

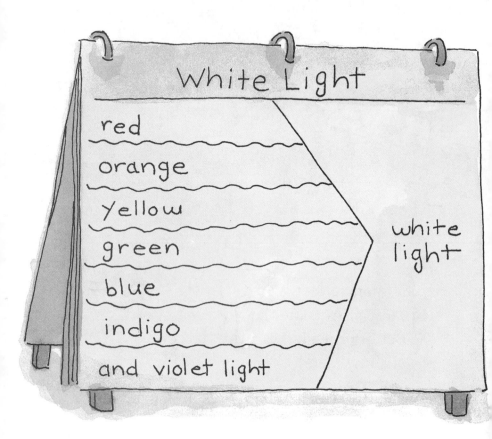

They are all mixed together.
That's what makes white light.

Pieces of glass, soap bubbles, and water
spray can split apart the white light.
Look closely and you'll always see
the same seven colors.
And always in the same order.

Light energy is at work in the supermarket.
You step up to the checkout.
The cashier slides your purchase over the counter.

Each item passes over a hole in the counter.
A thin, bright red light shines up through the hole.
You hear a beep.
The item's price appears on a screen.

The thin, bright light is called a laser.
It is a special kind of light.
Its beam is very powerful and very narrow.
The laser is far stronger and sharper
than ordinary light.
Some lasers are 1,000 times as bright as the sun!

Shine an ordinary flashlight on a dark night.
What happens?
The beam gets fainter and fainter the
farther it goes.
The light spreads out in a wide circle.
You can only see things that are close.

But not the laser.
You can see laser light for thousands of miles.
And it hardly spreads out at all.

In 1962, a laser was aimed at the moon.
The light was so bright people could see it from earth.
Yet the laser made a circle only 2½ miles across!

We've come a long way from candles to lasers.
Probably the future will be even "brighter."
Each day we learn more about light.
And about sound and heat, too!